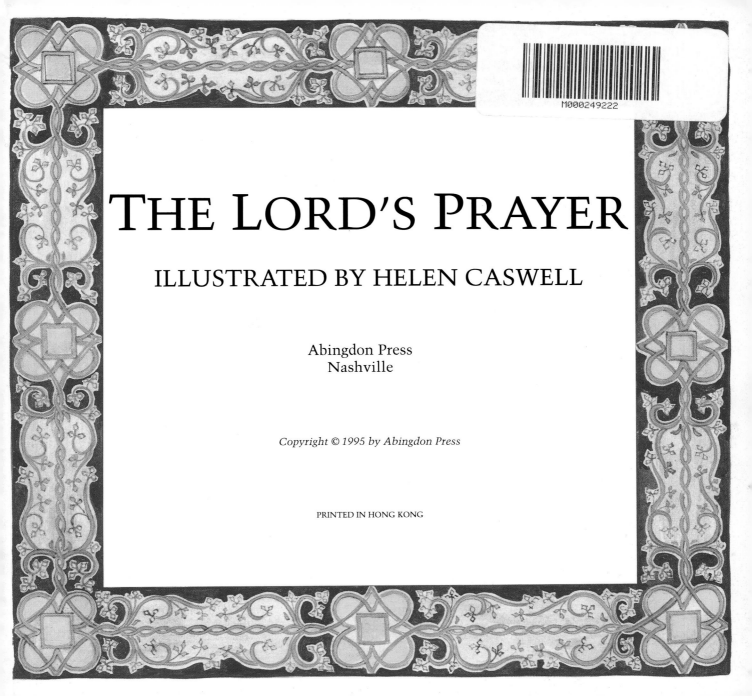

THE LORD'S PRAYER

ILLUSTRATED BY HELEN CASWELL

Abingdon Press
Nashville

PRINTED IN HONG KONG

Our Father,
who art in heaven,

allowed be
thy name.

Thy kingdom come,

hy will be done on earth as it is in heaven.

Give us this day
our daily bread.

And forgive us
our trespasses,
as we forgive those
who trespass
against us.

And lead us not
into temptation,

But deliver us
from evil.

For thine
is the kingdom,

And the power,

And the glory, forever.

Amen.